Walking With The Poor

- A 40-Day Devotional for the Spirit, Soul and Body

John Ashley Zimmerman

ISBN: 1523472391
ISBN-13: 978-1523472390

CONTENTS

About The Devotional

This devotional is written to facilitate a holistic discipline of spirit, soul and body. It includes a 40-day devotional to be read, followed by scripture and a personal challenge. The personal challenge is to be prayerfully considered while walking or participating in a similar physical activity (chair exercises can be found in the appendix). Hence, the holistic approach.

This holistic program can be a way to come together as an individual, small group, church/charge to better understand the issues of brokenness, poverty, hunger and homelessness. We affirm our faith regarding these issues so that we can more faithfully live the command found in Deut. 15:11:

"There will always be poor people in the land. Therefore I command you to be openhanded toward your fellow Israelites who are poor and needy in your land."

And when was it we saw you...

"The King will reply, 'Truly I tell you, whatever you did for one of the least of these brothers and sisters of mine, you did for me.'" (Matthew: 25:40)

Faith, Poverty and Fitness

Jesus said, "I am come that they might have life, and that they might have it more abundantly" (John 10:10). We all agree that, when Jesus said this, he was not teaching about a physical fitness program. It was about everlasting life. But it is also true that the "abundant life" Jesus offers has always included holistic well-being. The gospels repeatedly tell us that, wherever Jesus went, he worked miracles of healing of body, mind and spirit.

"Understanding poverty in all its dimensions (economic, political, cultural, physical, and spiritual), Wesley took the command of Jesus to minister to and live with the poor, with utter seriousness. For Wesleyans, aiding the poor means making them more capable to fulfill their God-given gifts; it does not mean making them dependent. Simply giving money, however important, will not release people from poverty unless the other dimensions of poverty are addressed. This means, of course, that the systems causing impoverished conditions must be changed. But it also means that disciples of Christ must be intimately related to the poor so that the poor can be fully brought into life-giving community. One of the most distinctive aspects of Wesley's teaching was that, while one cannot earn one's salvation, one's experience of the joy of salvation is to be found in the midst of what God is doing in and with the poor."
(*Poverty,* Wesleyan Core Term, The Wesley Study Bible, pg 247)

Discipline and devotion go hand in hand as we focus on our spirit, soul and personal health and recreation.

Week One

"The first person that I see on Ash Wednesday with a cross on their forehead always scares the living daylights out of me until I remember." -Unknown

Week 1 - Day 1

Ever since the reformation abandoned the act of impartation of ashes, Protestants have been hesitant to embrace the fullness of this first day of Lent. Few protestant churches offer Ash Wednesday gatherings; fewer offer the actual experience of the impartation of ashes; and even fewer individuals allow themselves to participate.

Every year I try to prepare myself for the unusual sight of seeing someone with a dirty smudge on their forehead. Yet, I am always taken by surprise and have to force myself to hide my stare. A cross made of ashes is a hideous sight on anyone's forehead.

Human nature does not naturally embrace sackcloth and ashes. We do all we can to deny our mortality, sinfulness and brokenness. We have the power to hide our own poverty through the mask of a smile, material possessions of affluence and appearances of perfection. Who wants to wear their wretchedness on their sleeve...or forehead?

This is the gift of Ash Wednesday. We cannot know Jesus as Savior if we don't recognize our need to be saved. Also, we cannot love our poor neighbor unless we acknowledge our own poverty.

As You Walk

"He raises the poor from the dust and lifts the needy from the ash heap." - Psalm 113:7

Dare to be honest and identify your own poverty. How are you poor in spirit ...relationships ...economically ...attitude ...mind ...emotion? Maybe the Spirit will lead you to swipe the dirt and touch your own forehead.

Week 1 - Day 2

The incarnation of Jesus Christ is God's most radical and perfect expression of relationship with a broken humanity. The very nature of his humble beginning reveals an identification with our brokenness to embark on a journey of liberation from the bonds of sin. The more elaborate, famous, wealthy and elitist the event; the more exclusive, untouchable and non-relational it becomes. God, however, reaches us on the most accessible level.

The Holy One purposely chose the setting of a stable as his first fleshly appearance. No throne or palace could accommodate both peasant and king. No other place on earth could be as accessible as a barn and a manger. From the moment of conception God sets the standard for relationship that includes all.

Throughout his earthly life Jesus relates to our own poverty. The King deserving of a palace chose homelessness; the Son of God chose to touch the leper; our Savior was pierced upon a cross. The earthly life of Jesus sets a precedent of intentional identification with our own wrecked life that tears down walls once impenetrable.

As You Walk

"God made him who had no sin to be sin for us, so that in him we might become the righteousness of God." - I Corinthians 5:21

In your meditation, approach Jesus not as the conquering King but as a suffering servant. See Him in the poverty He chose to embrace. Be open to discover new associations in how He relates to you in brokenness.

Week 1 - Day 3

My favorite childhood movie has to be the Wizard of Oz. As an adult I have come to find it a rich image of powerful human relationships.

Dorothy finds herself in a very foreign place. She is lost, desperately seeking her way home. In her fear of the unknown she is directed to the Wizard who can surely help her.

Along life's journey of following the yellow brick road she encounters the scarecrow; so different yet mysteriously similar in that they both need something. Dorothy locks arms and together they skip down the road. The story unfolds as they discover new unlikely friends sharing only one thing in common; all have a need and all can be set free by the Wizard.

The movie chronicles the journey of four characters who relate to each other in their poverty. There are joys, challenges and struggles that await around each turn of the road but, together, they overcome.

We each have a road to travel and God places divine encounters in our path. As we journey through life to the hope and salvation in Christ, we were never meant to be alone.

As You Walk

"But Ruth replied, "Don't urge me to leave you or to turn back from you. Where you go I will go, and where you stay I will stay. Your people will be my people and your God my God." - Ruth 1:16

Is your journey populated with diversity or have you left the tin man along the road paralyzed by tough circumstances of life?

Week 1 - Day 4

Decades ago my worship professor at seminary announced a shift in the liturgical year by declaring the Sunday before Easter as "Palm-Passion Sunday." Rather than singularly celebrating Palm Sunday, we need to include the observance of the Passion Week events leading to Easter.

His rationale was disappointing as he described the attendance behaviors of the current generation. The majority of our congregants no longer attend Maundy Thursday or Good Friday services. He aptly suggested that it would be a spiritual injustice for our personal worship journey to go from Palm Sunday directly to Easter. Therefore, we need to include the passion events within Palm Sunday.

While this shift of observance seeks to remedy a less-than-ideal reality, we should not lessen the significance of the last supper and the cross in our journey. The empty tomb of Easter cannot be fully realized without the cross.

The old rugged cross is not a pleasant sight. We would much rather rejoice at the entrance of the empty tomb. Yet the taste of the broken bread and pressed juice of the vine signals the veracity of our sinful nature and need for Jesus.

As You Walk

"Jesus looked at him and loved him. "One thing you lack," he said. 'Go, sell everything you have and give to the poor, and you will have treasure in heaven. Then come, follow me.'" – Mark 10:21

Do you follow Jesus out of convenience or sacrificial commitment?

Week 1 - Day 5

While taking on the fullness of humanity, Jesus maintained the completeness of his divinity. The cross that Jesus bore is not so much that he became poor, forsaking the privileges of divinity. Rather, the cross is about us becoming rich through Jesus choosing to walk with us in the resources of his riches. Our only hope of wholeness and restoration is at the mercy of God's heart.

An intentional search of the scriptures concerning God's outreach to the poor will reveal an amazing discovery into God's priorities. It becomes obvious that God is the defender of the poor. This is our Good News and sets the agenda that guides the Church.

I am reminded that I am blessed to be a blessing. This carries a responsibility to avail myself with a helping hand and share my unique resources that can serve those in need. Very rarely does one leave poverty without the support of someone outside of poverty. God has placed us in community so that we can support, help and encourage one another.

As You Walk

"He upholds the cause of the oppressed and gives food to the hungry. The Lord sets prisoners free, the Lord gives sight to the blind, the Lord lifts up those who are bowed down, the Lord loves the righteous. The Lord watches over the alien and sustains the fatherless and the widow, but he frustrates the ways of the wicked." -Psalm 146:7-9

When we could not come to God, God came to us. A person in poverty is waiting for you to choose to come and walk with them to wholeness. Hear the call.

Week 1 - Day 6

From the invention of the wheel to the modern day, we constantly strive to make life easier. We are surrounded with machines, gadgets and technology that tout a simpler life. It seems, however, that it has only served to make life more complicated.

Complexity requires resources of time, energy and possessions to supply its demand. We can get so involved in feeding our complex life that we have little room for spontaneity. In the story of the Good Samaritan, a priest and Levite could not deviate from their compounded life's agenda to provide aid. The appetite of complexity needs to be fed. We do not allow an occasion for God to lead us to the cries of the poor.

To simplify life is an exercise of freedom from the bondage of a seductive material world. Our hearts and minds become lighter from the load of concerns and cares that constantly follow a complex life. We grow closer to a reliance upon the strength of God.

Most importantly, a simpler life frees us to be available to the interruptions of those around us who need help, care and love. Relationship is able to be pursued and enjoyed to the glory of God.

As You Walk

"But a Samaritan, as he traveled, came where the man was; and when he saw him, he took pity on him. He went to him and bandaged his wounds, pouring on oil and wine. Then he put the man on his own donkey, brought him to an inn and took care of him." - Luke 10:33-34

What areas of your life can you begin to simplify? What steps can you take right now?

Week 1 - Day 7

At the foundation of love is free will. Love cannot be truly expressed unless we have the ability to choose the relationship. The very existence of the tree of the knowledge of good and evil was the essence of free will for Adam and Eve. God gave them the ability to choose a relationship or go off on their own and become like God. God has not created our relationship to be like puppets on a string that move only at His command. Love demands a freewill choice.

God is the perfect expression of love in that He possesses ultimate free will. His divine characteristics of omnipotence, omniscience and omnipresence give Him the free will to do anything. God has ultimate choice to do anything He wants and He has chosen to love us. What an expression of love!

Every day we, too, are given the free will to love God. We constantly choose to love Him, follow His commands and live a life pleasing to Him, or do our own thing. Even the people we encounter becomes a choice to love God in the way we respond. In no uncertain terms, God has revealed His expectation that when we walk with the poor in love and respect, we are choosing to love God.

As You Walk

"Dear friends, let us love one another, for love comes from God. Everyone who loves has been born of God and knows God. Whoever does not love does not know God, because God is love." - 1 John 4:7-8

In what ways do you consciously choose to love God by the way you serve others? When have you chose to "walk on the other side of the road" to avoid helping someone in need?

Walking/Activity Log for First Week

Day	*Activity*	*Minutes*	*Miles*	*Notes*
Sunday				
Monday				
Tuesday				
Wednesday				
Thursday				
Friday				
Saturday				

My Goals for the Week:

My Totals for the Week: (20 min. = 1 mile)

A Personal Story

Javon and Tenisha needed some help. The house they were renting was in foreclosure and they received an eviction notice. Javon could only find part-time work and Tenisha had been off for several weeks after giving birth to their third child.

They did not have the resources for a security deposit and first month's rent to secure another apartment. Javon, Tenisha and their three children stayed at The Refuge, an emergency shelter for homeless families, for about two months. Tenisha shared her thoughts on their time at our shelter.

"It has meant everything to us. Nothing would have been possible without the help of the (Refuge) staff. Without their referral, we would not have received the assistance from GECAC to help with our first month's rent and security deposit at our new apartment. The Refuge has given us diapers, clothes, food, and other items. They gave us Christmas presents. They provided transportation assistance. When our vehicle broke down they rescued us. They sent us with household items when we left."

"I wouldn't want to have gone anywhere else. They are very family oriented and Christian based, and I like that."

Second Week

"Our ministry to the poor becomes a means of grace by which God does His work of holiness in us. It becomes a way by which God perfects us in love and makes us Christ-like."

- John Wesley

Week 2 - Day 8

There are times we hesitate to specifically refer to poverty. A feeling of being judgmental can cause us to repress dialogue and shy from direct engagement ministry. We don't want to make people uncomfortable by identifying them as poor; hence, we pretend it does not exist thinking we are protecting persons from hurtful truth.

This would be a valid concern if our understanding of poverty came from a judgmental perspective. An attitude that we got it together denies our own identification with the fallen nature. If reference to the poor does not authentically include yourself, then it is a disparaging reference.

When we speak to poverty it is not the "other" but the "us." This frame of heart gives credibility to identify from a mutual perspective and respect. We do not speak to poverty from the top down, but from the pronouns of us and we.

As You Walk

"The Spirit of the Lord is on me, because he has anointed me to proclaim good news to the poor. He has sent me to proclaim freedom for the prisoners and recovery of sight for the blind, to set the oppressed free..." - Luke 4:18

"Poverty is the result of relationships that do not work, that are not just, that are not for life, that are not harmonious or enjoyable. Poverty is the absence of shalom in all its meanings."

(Bryant Myers, http://www.chalmers.org/poverty/definition)

In your own words, develop a holistic definition of poverty that includes yourself.

Week 2 - Day 9

As a follower of Christ we live in the tension of applying the commands of a disciplined walk without being judgmental. The Word of God truly is Good News that speaks life to a broken world, but we can easily become guilty of unqualified judgment.

Jesus clearly declares, "Do not judge, or you too will be judged. For in the same way you judge others, you will be judged, and with the measure you use, it will be measured to you." (Matt. 7:1-2) The straight and narrow path to which we commit our walk is the same path that we encourage others to follow; yet we are warned not to judge. The prophetic voice within the context of love and grace is a difficult dichotomy.

Everyone is responsible to their own journey. As we grow in our walk with the Lord we can be a model and encourage others, but ultimately we must yield responsibility to each individual. We release others to the same loving God who is patient and forgiving of our own faults; knowing only God can shepherd freedom.

As You Walk

"Why do you look at the speck of sawdust in your brother's eye and pay no attention to the plank in your own eye?" - Matthew 7:3

That person could put food on the table if they didn't spend so much money on cigarettes! This expression points to a common attitude we often encounter in our heart. Ask God to help you understand and show grace in light of the above scripture text.

Week 2 - Day 10

Sin is never pretty. In fact, it can be offensive and disgusting. The further we creep outside of our Christian circles, the more we may encounter persons who engage in behaviors, language, attitudes and actions that we deem offensive. Over time, the Church has let the "offense" of sin build "a fence" that separates us from being in the world.

The Church has become known for what it stands against and has lost the ability to lovingly engage a broken world. The fear of judgment from the world's perspective and the fear of offense from the Church's perspective has created wide boundaries.

Jesus refused to be offended when He touched the leper, ate with the tax collector and had his feet washed with the tears of a sinful women. Ultimately he willingly bore our sin as he embraced the cross. He crossed the boundary to stake the claim of the Kingdom.

We must be intentional to follow the example of Christ, and not let the offense of sin segregate us from a meaningful relationship with those who are not at the same place as us on the journey.

As You Walk

"My prayer is not that you take them out of the world but that you protect them from the evil one. They are not of the world, even as I am not of it." -*John 17:15-16*

We do well at not being of the world, but not so well at being in the world. How have you separated yourself from the world when God has actually given you opportunity to be light in the dark places?

Week 2 - Day 11

I was many miles away from home attending an inspirational conference when I was surprised to find someone from my area attending the same conference. Upon our greeting I made the comment, "We live so close yet have to travel 500 miles to see each other."

She replied, "Well, I just want to be where Jesus is."

Indeed the presence of Jesus was palpable at the conference but I couldn't help but wonder if I really needed to drive 500 miles to find Jesus. If I used the Gospels as a lead to discover the places Jesus frequented, I would be constantly drawn to the marginalized. If you want to find Jesus, look among those who exist on the fringes of society.

The mission of the church follows God's heart to the poor, lonely, unloved and outcast. We should not only be known for how we love each other but also how we love the other. Too often we find ourselves still locked in the upper room waiting to be sent. The Holy Spirit has come and the Voice says, "Go." Jesus is waiting to meet you with the least of these.

As You Walk

"Praise be to the God and Father of our Lord Jesus Christ, the Father of compassion and the God of all comfort, who comforts us in all our troubles, so that we can comfort those in any trouble with the comfort we ourselves have received from God." -II Cor. 1:3-4

The Christian chorus aptly sings, "And they'll know we are Christians by our love." If someone was looking for you, what is the likelihood they would find you among those Jesus frequented most?

Week 2 - Day 12

I often hear persons try to understand tragic events as somehow being in God's will. "God has a reason for everything," they explain. My theology, however, cannot be so simplified when I look into the face of a child so hungry that she confesses she could eat a rock. How could the will of God have a divine reason for a hungry child? ...or a bruised and battered spouse? ...a father out of control with an addiction? ...or a mother weeping over the tragic loss of her son to a brutal fight with cancer?

The prayer Jesus gave as a model for us to follow is what we call the Lord's Prayer. The second line prays, "Thy kingdom come. Thy will be done on earth, as it is in heaven." This prayer has been given to the Church because the perfect Kingdom of God is not fully realized on this side of heaven.

We acknowledge that kingdoms and principalities of darkness have established strongholds in which we must conquer in the name of Jesus. This becomes the mission of the Church as we are encouraged to pray and live that the perfect will and Kingdom life found in heaven be the very reality on earth.

As You Walk

"This, then, is how you should pray: "'Our Father in heaven, hallowed be your name, your kingdom come, your will be done, on earth as it is in heaven. Give us today our daily bread.'" - Matthew 6:9-13

Consider the people, places, things and systems within your reach that are outside the kingdom of God. How is God calling you to be God's light of love, hope, peace and salvation in these areas?

Week 2 - Day 13

Penn Jillette, of the magician duo, Penn & Teller, is a noted outspoken atheist. He has an interesting discussion on faith sharing. "If you believe that there's a heaven and a hell, and people could be going to hell or not getting eternal life, and you think that it's not really worth telling them this because it would make it socially awkward, how much do you have to hate somebody to *not* proselytize? How much do you have to hate somebody to believe everlasting life is possible and not tell them that?

"I mean, if I believed, beyond the shadow of a doubt, that a truck was coming at you, and you didn't believe that truck was bearing down on you, there is a certain point where I tackle you. And this is *more* important than that." Jillette is speaking to a foundational assumption of our Christian faith which is love.

It was God's love that sent His son Jesus to set us free from our poverty. Love is what fuels mission outreach in our churches and personal lives. The extent of how we serve those in poverty and share our faith to those who are lost is in direct proportion to how much we love them.

As You Walk

"For God so loved the world that he gave his one and only Son, that whoever believes in him shall not perish but have eternal life." - John 3:16

If the extent of your love is evidenced by the ways in which you serve the lost, broken and poor, how much do you love? In what ways can love motivate your acts of mercy?

Week 2 - Day 14

Mother Teresa writes, "One day an Australian man came and made a substantial donation. But as he did this he said, 'This is something external. Now I want to give something of myself.' Now he comes regularly to the house of the dying and gives not only his money but also his time.

I often ask for gifts that have nothing to do with money. There are so many other things one can give. What I desire is the presence of the donor, for him to touch those to whom he gives, to smile at them, for him to pay attention to them.

I never ask them for money or any material things. I ask them to bring their love, to offer the sacrifice of their hands. After some time they feel they belong to the poor and they are filled with the need to love. I think that a person who is attached to riches, is actually very poor."

Mother Teresa yearned for people to not give their money but to bring their money and invest with the ministry of presence among the poor. There is no substitute to the touch and face-to-face human interaction in ministry with the poor.

As You Walk

"My command is this: Love each other as I have loved you. Greater love has no one than this: to lay down one's life for one's friends.'" - John 15:12-13

Consider the ways in which you or your church works to alleviate suffering and poverty. Do they offer the ministry of presence? How can you change the ministries that simply offer gifts to ones that include interaction and relationship?

Walking/Activity Log for Second Week

Day	*Activity*	*Minutes*	*Miles*	*Notes*
Sunday				
Monday				
Tuesday				
Wednesday				
Thursday				
Friday				
Saturday				

My Goals for the Week:

My Totals for the Week: (20 min. = 1 mile)

A Personal Story

Thomas is a single father who stayed at The Refuge, an emergency shelter for homeless families, with his 3-year-old son. His own childhood was rather unstable after his alcoholic father left the family when he was 12-years-old. In the years that followed, Thomas turned to drugs, alcohol, gambling and crime . . . and found himself in juvenile detention and prison.

Thomas' turning point was meeting his newborn son in a prison family room. After his release, he needed to find shelter for himself and his son. He came to The Refuge, the only shelter in the city that could keep him and his son together in their own room.

"Little by little I'm starting to feel different," Thomas said of his stay at The Refuge. "First of all, it kept me and my son together. I didn't have to worry about that, so I could focus on moving forward with getting a job and finishing school. It means a lot to know that your son has a place to sleep, there's food and help with clothes and stuff. I wasn't worrying so much. I was able to get a part time job since I came here. The people at The Refuge really care about you, they listen to you, they pray with you. They help you find the resources that can help you move ahead."

Third Week

"While women weep, as they do now,
I'll fight
While little children go hungry, as they do now,
I'll fight
While men go to prison, in and out, in and out, as they do now,
I'll fight
While there is a drunkard left,
While there is a poor lost girl upon the streets,
While there remains one dark soul without the light of God,
I'll fight-I'll fight to the very end!"

— William Booth

Week 3 - Day 15

When we consider the relationship between the mission of the Church and the poor, the use of a preposition can change everything. A preposition is a word that governs a noun and establishes its relationship to another element. Identifying the mission of the Church as the noun, we will often use the preposition "to" to describe its relationship to the poor. Hence, we see the mission of the church directed to the poor. However, simply swapping "to" for the preposition "with" creates a profound shift in ministry.

The preposition "to" connotes a sense of giving from one who has to one who has not. Typically ministries *to* the poor include food pantries, Thanksgiving dinner baskets and coat drives in the winter. These are vital ministries, commanded in the scriptures, and usually accomplished well by the Church.

The preposition "with," however, governs the Church to walk alongside the poor in a deeper relationship. Ministry *with* the poor imparts a sense of mutual respect, fellowship and relationship at a transformational level. Ministry with the poor is not so common and popular in the Church. It requires a greater degree of commitment and humility.

As You Walk

"When Jesus reached the spot, he looked up and said to him, "Zacchaeus, come down immediately. I must stay at your house today." So he came down at once and welcomed him gladly." - Luke 19:5-6

List the ministries you or your church are involved in that are "to" and those that are "with" the poor. Are your lists out of balance?

Week 3 - Day 16

I love the opportunities to dwell in the unmistakable presence of Jesus. Worship is one of those means of presence. In my experience, it is during those holy moments of worship that I lose myself from this world and gaze into the eyes of Jesus. For this reason my heart longs to worship.

I have, however, encountered the presence of Jesus in what many would consider the most unlikely place...the poor. It should be no surprise, as the Bible plainly reveals, that we will find him as naked, hungry, lonely and in prison. Just like the two disciples on the road to Emmaus who encountered the resurrected Lord, my eyes have been opened to the mystery of his presence when I walk with the poor.

Following their Christ encounter, the two from Emmaus shared, "Were not our hearts burning within us while he talked with us on the road and opened the Scriptures to us?" (Luke 24:32) In the same way we find a strange familiarity that is the fragrance of Christ as we serve the poor.

As You Walk

"Then the righteous will answer him, 'Lord, when did we see you hungry and feed you, or thirsty and give you something to drink? When did we see you a stranger and invite you in, or needing clothes and clothe you? When did we see you sick or in prison and go to visit you?' "The King will reply, 'Truly I tell you, whatever you did for one of the least of these brothers and sisters of mine, you did for me.' – Matt. 25:37-40

Ask the same questions to your Lord, "When did we see you in need?" Where and who?

Week 3 - Day 17

Relief and development are two words used to guide ministry with the poor. We may understand the important differentiation of these words yet it often gets lost in practice. My experience with the Church is that we do very well with relief but have difficulty with development.

Relief is when things are given to help someone during times of tragedy and great difficulty. The Church is surely called to relief efforts and it is a fundamental expectation of its mission. Development is also an action of service yet denotes a process that can require greater commitment and sacrifice. The old proverb, "Give a person to fish, you feed them for a day; teach them to fish, you feed them for a lifetime" explains it well.

In many ways it is easier just to give the fish. Upon examination of the outreach efforts of the church, much more are relief efforts with few actually being mentoring and developmental. While relief is valid, we cannot be content to let it stand alone. The unique offering of the Church in a broken world is a commitment to development. The offering of your time, relationship, patience, and creativity requires a conscious decision to give of yourself. This is the example of Christ as he walked the earth.

As You Walk

"As iron sharpens iron, so one person sharpens another." - Proverbs 27:17

Who are you teaching to fish? Are there instances where you are giving fish for relief when you should be teaching a person to fish?

Week 3 - Day 18

In his earthly life we find the story of Jesus in Mark 5:21-43 who was summoned by a frantic father to come and heal his dying daughter. We can feel the tension as Jesus is making his way to Jairus' house pushing through the large crowd that pressed in against him.

God's Word gives us audience to a side story that is unfolding of which no one is aware. One soul who has no title, authority or status is buried deep in the crowd. She has been dealing with a bleeding issue for years and her last hope is walking past. Her great faith drives her to push through the crowd for just a touch of the hem of Jesus' garments. She knew this was enough for her relief from years of suffering.

Jesus stops! Within the urgency of a dying child, pleading father, and a host of other issues represented by the crowd, Jesus stops and asks, "Who touched me?"

The relieving power that poured out was not sufficient for the heart of Jesus. He could not be satisfied to continue down the road without knowing who touched him. He needed to establish relationship. Preserved in the Holy Scriptures for all of earthly time, the Church is powerfully reminded that the urgency of relief cannot neglect the transformational potential of relationship.

As You Walk

"But Jesus said, "Someone touched me; I know that power has gone out from me." - Luke 8:46

The noise of the world muffles the cries of the voiceless. God calls you to tune your ears to those who are lost in the crowd. Ask God to open your heart to grow closer to the poor.

Week 3 - Day 19

Acts 9 chronicles the conversion experience of Paul as we see Saul (the former name of Paul) on his way to Damascus with the authority to arrest Christians. Saul has proved his murderous threats to be taken seriously and word of his mission spread. We witness, however, the work of the Holy Spirit on the road to Damascus as Saul encounters God.

In a parallel story the Spirit is also prepping and empowering Ananias to meet Saul when he arrives. Ananias, understandably, is not fully willing to confront Saul. He knows what Saul has done in the past and what he is has come to do to the disciples. Ananias could only look at Saul through his history.

The Spirit's words to Ananias where powerful, "Go! This man is my chosen instrument to proclaim my name..." God blessed Ananias to believe in Saul not through his history but in light of his destiny. Empowered by destiny Ananias meets Saul and greets him with, "Brother Saul."

The ways of the world treat others according to their history, but the ways of the Kingdom call us to see others for their destiny of wholeness and relationship with Jesus Christ. This is the hope of the Church that is grounded upon the miraculous ability of God to lift us beyond our history.

As You Walk

"Placing his hands on Saul, he said, "Brother Saul, the Lord—Jesus...has sent me so that you may see again and be filled with the Holy Spirit." *- Acts 9:17*

Ask God to change your perspective of the poor to see others the way God sees them. Allow God to reveal the places you struggle to get past a person's history.

Week 3 - Day 20

During a post-resurrection appearance among His disciples, Jesus issued what we call the "great commission." The most popular version of the "go into all the world" great commission is found in Matthew 28. It is, however, also written in Mark's Gospel that we less frequent.

Mark 16:15-18 reads, "He said to them, "Go into all the world and preach the gospel to all creation. Whoever believes and is baptized will be saved, but whoever does not believe will be condemned. And these signs will accompany those who believe: In my name they will drive out demons; they will speak in new tongues; they will pick up snakes with their hands; and when they drink deadly poison, it will not hurt them at all; they will place their hands on sick people, and they will get well."

I suspect one of the reasons we avoid the Mark 16 version is the reference to challenging ministry conditions that include demons, snakes, poison and sickness. Jesus is preparing His disciples for difficult ministry.

The challenges of ministry today are no different. We need to welcome and submit to the power of the Holy Spirit for victory in ministry. Then, these signs will also follow us.

As You Walk

"Very truly I tell you, whoever believes in me will do the works I have been doing, and they will do even greater things than these, because I am going to the Father." - John 14:12

Are you open to allow the Holy Spirit to lead you into challenges greater than yourself?

Week 3 - Day 21

We have become hypersensitive to the respect of personal space, boundaries and privacy. We are accustomed to sitting back and awaiting the invitation or thinking that we are not welcomed. Not wanting to be accused of the bad word of "proselytizing" or the non-politically correct actions of forcing our faith, we hide in the shadows waiting for an invitation.

This attitude, however, is often challenged by the life of Jesus. Concerning His relationship with the poor, He never waited for an invitation. The conditions of poverty always provide an open invitation for love, care and support. Jesus acted upon the poverty of Zacchaeus' spirit to invite himself over for dinner. A sinful women acted upon the invitation of her own spiritual poverty to enter the Pharisee's house and fall at His feet. Simon did not invite her to his house, but the heart of Jesus welcomed her.

We are wary of the continual misconception of the mantra, "separation of church and state." As such, we are missing the open invitation to share the love of God. All through Scripture the God of this universe continually affirms the invitation to enter the broken world with the transformational power of the Gospel. The Spirit goes before us opening the doors for your love to make a difference.

As You Walk

"When Jesus reached the spot, he looked up and said to him, "Zacchaeus, come down immediately. I must stay at your house today." So he came down at once and welcomed him gladly." - Luke 19:5-6

Where are the places of the poor, broken, disengaged and lost that you have not visited? ...You have an open invitation.

Walking/Activity Log for Third Week

Day	*Activity*	*Minutes*	*Miles*	*Notes*
Sunday				
Monday				
Tuesday				
Wednesday				
Thursday				
Friday				
Saturday				

My Goals for the Week:

My Totals for the Week: (20 min. = 1 mile)

A Personal Story

Ed is a 57-year-old Veteran who lives out his "attitude of gratitude" through self-sufficiency, kindness, generosity and volunteerism . . . but it has been a journey for this one-time homeless Veteran and former Liberty House resident. Liberty House is a transitional shelter program for homeless Veteran men.

It was not always an easy road, and although it took more than one "tour" at Liberty House, Ed credits the Liberty House program for giving him the action plan to a better life. "Living with several other men presented challenges, but Liberty House was a mixture of all different types of people," Ed said. "We learned to help one another and respect each other."

Since completing the program, Ed has purchased and paid off a vehicle, has his own apartment, a steady income, and mended relationships with his family members. "I'm on the road to recovery and I'm very happy and most definitely grateful for everything they have helped me with," he added.

Fourth Week

"Being unwanted, unloved, uncared for, forgotten by everybody, I think that is a much greater hunger, a much greater poverty than the person who has nothing to eat.."

- Mother Theresa

Week 4 - Day 22

One day an expert in the law wanted to know what he must do to inherit eternal life. Jesus replied in terms that spoke to the priorities of an expert in the law. He shared the commands to love God and love your neighbor. In an attempt to legalistically define discipleship the expert further questioned, "Who is my neighbor?" Here is where Jesus tells the story of the good Samaritan. Jesus adds the flesh of relationship to the bones of the law.

Jesus helps the man understand his neighbor as whoever crosses our daily path. For many of our neighbors, a simple greeting and smile is the expression of love that adequately fulfills the command to love. There are neighbors that we meet, however, that require a greater expression of love in action.

These are the neighbors who surround us filled with hurt, pain and left on the side of our cultural road to be ignored. To these neighbors the expression of love requires a greater level of sacrifice and commitment. It becomes convenient to keep our eyes looking straight ahead and "miss" those in need as we pass.

As You Walk

"Which of these three do you think was a neighbor to the man who fell into the hands of robbers?" The expert in the law replied, "The one who had mercy on him." Jesus told him, "Go and do likewise." – Luke 10:36-37

Within your proximity today are persons who are hurt, beat up and bleeding from life. Ask God to open your eyes to see and your heart to act as an expression of God's love.

Week 4 - Day 23

I am not a cat person but living in my neighborhood is a cat that has to visit me regularly. I tried ignoring her but slowly I softened and started to interact and let her into my space. Soon I learned her name and started to recognize her unique character.

A thing called relationship developed that changed my reference to the cat from an impersonal "it" to an affectionate "Taffy." "A rose by any other name would smell as sweet" is a commonly quoted part of a dialogue in William Shakespeare's play Romeo and Juliet. In this play Juliet argues that the names of things do not matter, only what things "are."

One can never smell the flower from a distance. You must get close to smell its sweet fragrance. Likewise, when we choose to keep distance between all of God's people, we only perpetuate stereotypes and prejudices. Every person, by virtue of being knit together by the hands of God, is a rose.

We must choose to grow in relationship with those that seem so different. It is there that we smell the sweet fragrance of God's creation. Trust the strength of relationship to take you past your barriers to share the transforming love of God.

As You Walk

"And if you greet only your own people, what are you doing more than others? Do not even pagans do that? Be perfect, therefore, as your heavenly Father is perfect." - Matthew 5:46-48

Identify the barriers that we use to keep us separate from those whose life seems different. In what ways can you break down those barriers and experience others made in the image of God?

Week 4 - Day 24

Charles Ramsey was the Cleveland man who put down his Big Mac to help rescue three women who were kidnapped and held captive for years. Following a TV news interview with Ramsey, the country quickly discovered his brilliant insight and experience as he bluntly offered opinions on race, class and life in the inner city.

Relating to the rescue, a particularly unfiltered yet brilliant statement speaks wisdom as he said, "When a little pretty white girl ran into a black man's arms, something was wrong."

Tragedy and hardship is the most authentic unifier we experience. Barriers, boundaries and walls are transparent among those in crisis. Race, class, life circumstances and other dividers diminish when we are faced with crisis and need. Before we experience the common Savior through Jesus Christ for the world, we must first recognize the urgent plight of our common human condition.

As is experienced during every crisis, we truly walk equal ground as we help one another to safety. The differences that were once deemed important mysteriously vanish as we assist and be assisted along the rocky journey of life.

As You Walk

"For God so loved the world that he gave his one and only Son, that whoever believes in him shall not perish but have eternal life." - John 3:16

Take this time to celebrate the voice of the Rescuer who calls your name. Commit to reach out to another along your path who needs your encouragement, strength and hope to be set free.

Week 4 - Day 25

Sometimes we can get overwhelmed by the depth of poverty we encounter. Whether in our own lives or the world around us we can quickly succumb to hopelessness. While God has created us with human resources of skills, talents, gifts, time and creativity, we are still faced with a deficit to overcome. A constant failure to rise above may result in surrender.

Our mission to release oppression, however, is not a human mission. It is a commission that originates from within the Kingdom of God; and included with the mandate are God's full resources. We gravitate, however, to rely too heavily upon ourselves and neglect an expectation of the miraculous through the Holy Spirit.

In Luke 9 the story is told of a father who brought his demon-possessed son to Jesus. The mere act of coming to Jesus expresses a certain amount of faith yet the father hints of concern whether Jesus can heal his son. Even though the father believes, he still seeks to grow deeper in his faith. Of course we know the end of the story...the son is healed and the father's faith is deepened to know that the miraculous is within the resources of the Kingdom.

As You Walk

"But if you can do anything, take pity on us and help us." "If you can'?" said Jesus. "Everything is possible for one who believes." Immediately the boy's father exclaimed, "I do believe; help me overcome my unbelief!" - Mark 9:22-24

Acknowledge your limitations and open your heart to the fullness of the Holy Spirit. Let God transform your areas of unbelief into hopeful expectation.

Week 4 - Day 26

To look at a picture of a sunrise, it would be hard to determine if it was a sunrise or a sunset as they can look identical. The differences, however, are quite remarkable. A sunset marks the end while a sunrise heralds new beginnings. Through the hope of God we have the privilege to choose the sunrise over the sunset.

In the assembly room of Independence Hall in Philadelphia, George Washington sat in what is now called the "rising sun chair." Carved into that chair is a sun with radiating beams from the horizon. Benjamin Franklin is credited with saying, during the signing of the Constitution, that he has great happiness to know that it is a rising and not a setting sun.

Lenten contemplations can remind us of the setting sun and the mortality of our surroundings. We are, however, people of a rising sun. There are promises of God that give us the hope of restoration and newness. Even when life seems to deliver setting sun experiences, the resurrection life of Christ can turn your sunsets into sunrises with promises of new beginnings that cannot be foretold. The invitation of our Lord is to commitment our sunsets to his Son rise.

As You Walk

"He is like the light of morning at sunrise on a cloudless morning, like the brightness after rain that brings grass from the earth." - II Samuel 23:4

Identify the setting sun experiences that threaten you and/or those around you. Pray that God will reverse the trend and yield your life to be instruments of the sunrise.

Week 4 - Day 27

During the time of Christopher Columbus, people were very interested in finding a sailing route around Africa to China, Japan and India. They believed they would find expensive jewels and riches. The experts believed that sailing east was the best route. Columbus, however, argued that sailing in the opposite direction would get them to these lands much faster.

Columbus daringly set sail with three ships, the Nina, Pinta and Santa Maria and about 90 men. On October 12, 1942 Columbus landed on an island southeast of Florida. He claimed this island for Spain and named it the Indies, since he thought he had landed in India.

While, technically, the adventurous spirit of Columbus led him to failure, one cannot argue the overwhelming success of the mission. He did not find the indented trade route but what he did discover was far better. This is often the experience of the adventurer.

God expects us to be spiritually adventurous as well. He leads us to places we have never been and expects us to share the glorious faith. In fact, there are blessings of fruit that await us that we do not even know exist!

As You Walk

"For the Spirit God gave us does not make us timid, but gives us power, love and self-discipline."

- II Timothy 1:7

Evaluate the level of adventure in your spirit. Are you willing to go even to the unknown places?

Week 4 - Day 28

Prayerfully consider these words from Isaiah. Be open to let the ancient text confront your present walk with God. From Isaiah 58:4-7:

"You cannot fast as you do today
and expect your voice to be heard on high. Is this the kind of fast I have chosen,
only a day for people to humble themselves?
Is it only for bowing one's head like a reed
and for lying in sackcloth and ashes?
Is that what you call a fast,
a day acceptable to the Lord?
Is not this the kind of fasting I have chose:
to loose the chains of injustice
and untie the cords of the yoke,
to set the oppressed free
and break every yoke?
Is it not to share your food with the hungry
and to provide the poor wanderer with shelter—
when you see the naked, to clothe them,
and not to turn away from your own flesh and blood?

God's chosen fast is a self denial that calls us to meet the poor. The fast that pleases God produces tangible results of freedom for the oppressed.

As You Walk

"'He defended the cause of the poor and needy, and so all went well. Is that not what it means to know me?' declares the LORD." - Jeremiah 22:16

According to Isaiah, what kind of fasting is evident in your life? Take time to repent if your fasting is found not to be pure.

Walking/Activity Log for Fourth Week

Day	*Activity*	*Minutes*	*Miles*	*Notes*
Sunday				
Monday				
Tuesday				
Wednesday				
Thursday				
Friday				
Saturday				

My Goals for the Week:

My Totals for the Week: (20 min. = 1 mile)

A Personal Story

Sometimes, it's the small kindnesses that make the greatest impact.

I work with Project Hope Outreach, an on-the-street ministry to the homeless community. We meet with and talk to homeless individuals and families - in shelters, soup kitchens, public places, and on the street. Last year, we worked with 277 people in need.

The type of help we can offer varies – bus tokens to get to doctor's appointments and job interviews; information on where to find assistance; emergency hotel stays; help in securing identification paperwork and birth certificates. We may see an individual only once, some we have established a rapport with over several years.

In my job, I think the biggest impact we can have is to listen. Some of these folks have multiple issues that keep them from independence and self-sufficiency. Many are desperate and depressed. Most just need to know that someone cares. That is where hope comes in - and when there is hope, there are possibilities.

Fifth Week

"We must talk about poverty, because people insulated by their own comfort lose sight of it."

- Dorothy Day

Week 5 - Day 29

As a disciple of Christ we cannot underestimate the ministry of presence. Everywhere we go we bring the radiance, expectation, and authority of Christ. As Jesus has come to proclaim good news to the poor, God has designed redemption to be carried on by the Church. In the name of Jesus and the power of the Holy Spirit the Church is called to be the redeeming presence of God among the poor and broken.

There is no substitute to the responsibility of relationship unto which we are called. While we find accountability, growth and fellowship when we gather within our church family, we cannot grow comfortable to continually exist within these familiar settings. God has empowered and expects us to avail ourselves outside the Christian walls we can conveniently build around ourselves.

We are blessed with the availability of Bible studies, worship and Christian fellowship. Our opportunity to grow deeper in theology and personal relationship with Christ is unprecedented. This, however, can become an impediment to allowing ourselves to be sent to people and places where we may not find immediate comfort and ease. God calls us out to be God's representative voice and heart in the broken places of this world.

As You Walk

"For where two or three gather in my name, there am I with them." - Matthew 18:20

Ask God to reveal the call in your life to people and places that require you to cross over borders of comfort and familiarity. Choose to be the presence of God's hope extending the wholeness of the Kingdom.

Week 5 - Day 30

We all desire to grow in our relationship with the Lord and as a disciple of Christ. We know that we have not reached perfect love so we seek opportunities to learn and practice the image of God. We live a lifelong journey of discovery as we can uncover new insights about god and humanity every time we visit the Bible. There are, however, blind spots in our spiritual life that can go undetected.

A driver of a car must identify blind spots in the side view mirror. Once exposed, we know to purposefully look for what we may have missed seeing. The danger is when we fail to acknowledge the possibility of blind spots and never adjust. Similarly there may be spiritual blind spots that we have not known to exist.

Blind spots are not readily exposed through traditional means of discipleship growth. They are hidden behind a worldview that defines how we interpret the scriptures. We must be willing to acknowledge the presence of blind spots and seek God to reveal them to us.

In walking with the poor, our failures are not that we are turning a blind eye to the poor but that we have blind spots in relationship that we do not know exist.

As You Walk

"The LORD said to him, "Who gave human beings their mouths? Who makes them deaf or mute? Who gives them sight or makes them blind? Is it not I, the LORD?
- Exodus 4:11

Ask God to reveal your blind spots concerning ministry with the poor. Take action on God's leading.

Week 5 - Day 31

As I child I would hear the saying, "Sticks and stones may break my bones but names will never hurt me." This would be shared as a defense to names and ridicule that a child may endure. I have since learned that this phrase could not be further from the truth. Words have the power to create and destroy at levels we may not fully realize.

The power of the spoken word was demonstrated at creation when God spoke and it was done. This creative word has been given to us as well. Simple words of encouragement and life can contribute to strong foundations. Unfortunately, the hearts and minds of many have been hurt by words of destruction that have filled their lives.

When we walk with the poor we are within the proximity to speak encouragement, hope and support into hearts. The creative power of life-giving words can positively influence someone for a lifetime. To have someone counter the lies of Satan who desires to steal, kill and destroy can be the voice of truth others so desperately need to hear.

Words of life are not empty words cheaply available and delivered but are based upon the promises of God that are "yes" and "amen."

As You Walk

"With the tongue we praise our Lord and Father, and with it we curse human beings, who have been made in God's likeness. Out of the same mouth come praise and cursing. My brothers and sisters, this should not be." - James 3:9

Pray for sensitivity and commitment to fill every context of your presence with words of life.

Week 5 - Day 32

Acts 10 records the conversion of the first Gentile to the gospel of Christ in the person of Cornelius, a Caesarean army officer, a centurion. This was a man of a good reputation as well as powerful military rank.

Up to this point the apostles and the initial converts maintained their Jewish bias against all Gentiles and considered them unworthy of a relationship with God, and certainly not with themselves, as the Jews were the chosen people of God. This bias was misapplied, but God had a plan to overcome their prejudice through Peter. He had to reach within himself to go to the home of a Gentile.

The social ramifications of Peter entering the home of Cornelius were revolutionary. Only the direct operation of the Holy Spirit was sufficient to convince Peter that God endorsed their presence in that home and the preaching of the gospel to Gentiles.

It matters not if you are a white, middle-class businessperson in the 'Bible belt' of the United States or a jungle dweller in Africa or South America, or a veiled Arabian woman in Kuwait, the principle of Acts 10:35 applies.

As You Walk

"Then Peter began to speak: "I now realize how true it is that God does not show favoritism but accepts from every nation the one who fears him and does what is right. – Acts 10:34-35

Consider the circle of friends and relationships with whom you surround yourself. Does it reflect a diversity that mirrors the heart of God or give evidence of a bias that limits your love?

Week 5 - Day 33

The comparison of a cruise ship to a rescue vessel can help us better understand the mission of the church.

For many, the church is like a luxury liner. It exists for the comfort of the passengers and centers life on caring for the needs of its occupants. We seek inspirational worship and sermons that satisfy us through the week. Our covered dish dinners showcase the best recipes and fellowship. We have comfortably settled into the pew that has become our designated seat.

Jesus and the early disciples, however, have clearly identified the mission of the Church that more resembles a rescue vessel. The rescue vessel exists to save and set free those in life threatening circumstances. The equipment, training and destination of the crew are all about those who are in need.

The crew of the rescue vessel cares about one another and ensures their safety and wellbeing, but all for the common mission. It is the cry of the needy for whom they attune their heart and stand ready for the call. The crew finds no greater fulfillment than when they are on a mission.

As You Walk

"I was eyes to the blind and feet to the lame. I was a father to the needy; I took up the case of the stranger. I broke the fangs of the wicked and snatched the victims from their teeth." - Job 29:15-17

What ship does your church most resemble? What is the mission of the crew to which you belong?

Week 5 - Day 34

We live in a broken world. All around us, and even within, there is evidence of lost hope, shattered dreams and broken lives. Sin that was introduced at the fall of creation continues to pervert humanity from the righteousness and wholeness in our relationship with God. All of creation is in disharmony.

Poverty can be understood as a descriptive term for every level of disharmony. Everything we lack for completeness is a form of poverty. No one escapes its grasp in some form or another. Jesus has come as the Great Reconciler of all that separates. Poverty is vanquished in the presence of God. As it is written in II Corinthians 5:17, "Therefore, if anyone is in Christ, the new creation has come: The old has gone, the new is here! All this is from God, who reconciled us to himself through Christ..."

As a reconciled people, this passage continues to call us to mission. II Corinthians 5:18 continues, "and [Christ] gave us the ministry of reconciliation: that God was reconciling the world to himself in Christ, not counting people's sins against them. And he has committed to us the message of reconciliation."

We are mandated to seek out those who have been marginalized, divided and separated and share the transforming truths of the Gospel in word and deed. There is no other person or group in this world that has the true message of reconciliation.

As You Walk

"We are therefore Christ's ambassadors, as though God were making his appeal through us." II Cor 25:20

Identify the people and places that are not reconciled to Kingdom life. What is your message?

Week 5 - Day 35

We use labels to help define and understand one another. While labels can attempt to clarify individuals, they often become a stereotypical shortcut that falls short of true understanding. The Church has its share of labels that include descriptions of theological stance and priorities of faith expressions that serve more to divide than clarify.

We apply labels such as conservative, liberal, evangelical, social justice, charismatic, fundamental, reconciling, contemporary and traditional to replace the more demanding action of relationship. We talk about a theological stance and fail to recognize the heart and soul that is behind the label. It is too easy to dehumanize the person who appears to be unlike yourself by placing them into your predefined label.

Along my journey I continually learn that theology, doctrine and practice exists more in the center than the extremes. When we listen to those whom we have labeled as different from us, we begin to glean elements of diversity that strengthen us.

In the book of Acts the Jews struggled to accept Gentiles as authentic recipients of the grace of God. The ultimate recognition of the Gentile was through a relational experience that began with Peter. His personal experience could not be discounted and the barriers of labels were overcome.

As You Walk

"The circumcised believers who had come with Peter were astonished that the gift of the Holy Spirit had been poured out even on Gentiles." - Acts 10:45

With what theological labels do you most identify? Purposely seek to understand others who are outside our own labels.

Walking/Activity Log for Fifth Week

Day	*Activity*	*Minutes*	*Miles*	*Notes*
Sunday				
Monday				
Tuesday				
Wednesday				
Thursday				
Friday				
Saturday				

My Goals for the Week:

My Totals for the Week: (20 min. = 1 mile)

Sixth Week

"Poverty calls us to sow hope.... Poverty is the flesh of the poor Jesus, in that child who is hungry, in the one who is sick, in those unjust social structures."
- Pope Francis

Week 6 - Day 36

Mark Altrogge wrote a song and the chorus sings, "I have a destiny I know I shall fulfill. I have a destiny in that city on a hill. I have a destiny and it's not an empty wish for I know I was born for such a time as this." (I Have a Destiny © 1986 People of Destiny International/Word Music).

There is a freeing comfort to know our future eternal destiny lies in the arms of our Shepherd who keeps us through the ages. The freedom gained from knowing our eternal destiny is practiced through courage, commitment and sacrifice to also submit our temporal earthly life to God's destiny.

Esther accepted her earthly destiny through the encouragement of Mordecai and brought deliverance to her people. To walk in her destiny Esther had to trust, risk, and accept God's divine purpose for her life.

We cannot live our Spirit-filled destiny only in the realm of a future hope of heaven. God has given us a destiny for today that is unique to each of us. The Samaritan accepted his destiny when he came upon one beaten. The widow accepted her destiny to feed Elijah even with scarce resources. You have been given a destiny for such a time as this.

As You Walk

"You did not choose me, but I chose you and appointed you so that you might go and bear fruit—fruit that will last—and so that whatever you ask in my name the Father will give you. – John 15:16

Ask God for a heart to seek, eyes to see, commitment to lead and courage to walk in your destiny, as an ambassador of love and compassion, with those is poverty.

Week 6 - Day 37

We are immersed in a culture of instant gratification. Everything from the microwave to the internet has caused us to expect what we want when we want it. Fad diets and get-rich-quick schemes draw our interest. I once microwaved instant coffee and was annoyed by how long it took.

We can be deceived to expect results much more quickly than is realistic and become complacent to believe success has been achieved. This influences our relationship as a disciple of Jesus Christ. We drop the canned item into the basket and think we have conquered hunger and donate the blanket to the shelter and think we have alleviated homelessness.

The reality, however, is that very little of our Christian discipleship is achieved quickly. Words such as process, growth and journey are more relevant to the Christian life. Taking up our cross to follow Christ is, by the very essence of being Christian, a commitment to sacrifice of time, energy, emotion and resources. Our walk with the poor is not a microwaveable action but a journey that unfolds throughout a lifetime.

As You Walk

"Jesus asked, "Do you see anything?" He looked up and said, "I see people; they look like trees walking around." Once more Jesus put his hands on the man's eyes. Then his eyes were opened, his sight was restored, and he saw everything clearly." -Mark 8:23-25

Are you in ministry to the poor or with the poor? How do your expectations need to change?

Week 6 - Day 38

Our view of the cross today is so different from the perspective of the early disciples. The first Christians only knew the cross as a brutal instrument of crucifixion. It was feared and represented the ultimate of shame and scorn.

Today, however, the cross has been inseparably paired with redemption through Jesus Christ which reduces its offense. It has become the subject of favorite hymns; jewelry of many styles, gems and precious metals; and the subject of art that hangs on our walls.

Consequently, when Jesus commands to take up our cross and follow Him, generations receive it differently. To the early Christian, this was unmistakably a call to total surrender. Few of us, however, shudder at the thought like the original hearer.

The depth of sacrifice contained in such a command has not lessened. We must intentionally strive to yield daily to the call of self denial and the intensity to embrace our cross. As we do, the surprising peace and quiet comfort is found through expressions of love with the poor.

As You Walk

"Then Jesus told his disciples, "If anyone would come after me, let him deny himself and take up his cross and follow me. [25] For whoever would save his life[a] will lose it, but whoever loses his life for my sake will find it. - Matthew 16:24-25

Ask God to reveal areas of your life where you have neglected your cross.

Week 6 - Day 39

"Open doors" is the closing proclamation of the slogan that brands the United Methodist Church. It serves as an invitation to the entire world that they are welcome. I cannot imagine a congregation that, at least verbally, does not want people to come to church.

We give attention to radical hospitality, programming, public relations and seeker-sensitivity to present our church as inviting and open to the newcomer. Members are constantly encouraged to invite friends, neighbors, co-workers and family members to attend church.

We have a strong "come to church" emphasis but I have to search long and hard to find this emphasis in the heart of Jesus and his message to the Church. Conversely the message of Jesus and the example of the early church is a "go to" emphasis. God calls us to go into the world and share God's peace, hope and love with the poor through mission and service.

We cannot expect anyone to come into the church until we first get out of the church and meet one another in the love of Jesus. Before the doors of the church open inward, they must first open outward leading us to the hopeless, homeless, and disengaged.

As You Walk

"He said to them, 'Go into all the world and preach the gospel to all creation.'" - Mark 16:15

Take this time to evaluate the pattern of your witness. Are you a "come to" or a "go to" Christian? Commit your time and service to agencies and ministries that enable you to go and make disciples.

Week 6 - Day 40

Walking with the poor always requires a self-denial and commitment that is at the heart of unselfishness. There is a consumption of time, energy and resources that can cause us to question whether we can serve in such a capacity. When we count the cost, sometimes we see a cross before us that is waiting to be picked up. Are we willing?

A spiritual truth that can only be fully understood by actual experience is that we have been given a mission with the poor. And that mission brings the greatest fulfillment and joy to our lives. I have found that my happiest moments are when God is using me to bless another.

This promise is what Isaiah declares in the sharing of this promise from the 58th chapter.
He declares that when you walk with the poor, "...then your light will rise in the darkness, and your night will become like the noonday. The Lord will guide you always; he will satisfy your needs in a sun-scorched land and will strengthen your frame.

You will be like a well-watered garden, like a spring whose waters never fail. Your people will rebuild the ancient ruins and will raise up the age-old foundations; you will be called Repairer of Broken Walls, Restorer of Streets with Dwellings."

As You Walk

What do these promises mean to you? Are you willing to commit your life to walk with the poor, broken and lost? Open your heart to be a person who is known as the "Repairer of Broken Walls."
... You have spent 40 days considering the Scriptures and growing in the heart of God.

Now it is time to go!

Walking/Activity Log for Sixth Week

Day	*Activity*	*Minutes*	*Miles*	*Notes*
Sunday				
Monday				
Tuesday				
Wednesday				
Thursday				
Friday				
Saturday				

My Goals for the Week:

My Totals for the Week: (20 min. = 1 mile)

APPENDIX

Chair Exercises

Chair exercises are gentle on the body and are generally safe for most people to do. You are not likely to injure yourself doing any of these exercises, however it's always good to check with your doctor before beginning a new exercise program.
All of the exercises below should be performed in a straight chair. Sit up straight in the chair with your feet flat on the floor, unless otherwise directed.

Stretches

1. Begin with head in normal position.
2. Turn head to right, as though looking over the right shoulder.
3. Turn head toward the left. Repeat slowly 10 times.

~~~~~~~~~~~~~~~~~~~~~~~~~~~~~~~~~~~~~~

1. Begin with head in normal position, looking forward.
2. Shrug shoulders up toward ears.

~~~~~~~~~~~~~~~~~~~~~~~~~~~~~~~~~~~~~~

Hand Grip

1. Hold a tennis ball in each hand.
2. Slowly squeeze the ball as hard as you can and hold it for 3-5 seconds.
3. Relax the squeeze slowly.
4. Repeat 10-15 times. Return to starting position. Repeat slowly 10 times.

~~~~~~~~~~~~~~~~~~~~~~~~~~~~~~~~~~~~~~

1. Hands to shoulders, elbows out.
2. Bring elbows together. Repeat slowly 10 times.

~~~~~~~~~~~~~~~~~~~~~~~~~~~~~~~~~~~~~~

1. Give yourself a hug, crossing arms at shoulder level.
2. Now pat yourself on the back!
3. Lean to the left.

4. Lean to the right!
5. Hold each position for a slow count of 10 seconds then release.

~~~~~~~~~~~~~~~~~~~~~~~~~~~~~~~~~~~

Breast Stroke

1. Bring hands together, chest level.
2. Move hands out and around to side.
3. Repeat slowly 10 times.

~~~~~~~~~~~~~~~~~~~~~~~~~~~~~~~~~~~

1. Stretch legs out front.
2. Flutter kick 10 times.
3. Now scissors kick, crossing ankles side to side. Repeat 10 times.

~~~~~~~~~~~~~~~~~~~~~~~~~~~~~~~~~~~

1. Extend one leg.
2. Circle ankle 10 times.
3. Opposite direction 10 times
4. Flex and point toe 10 times. Repeat series with the other leg.

~~~~~~

Exercises with Therabands

1. If you have a theraband, hold the theraband with one end in each hand.
2. Put foot in center of band and stretch foot out.
3. Lift foot with theraband
4. Hold for slow count of 10.
5. Repeat with other leg.

~~~~~~

Theraband Biceps

1. Put one end of band under right foot, right elbow on knee.
2. Pull band toward right shoulder. Repeat 10 times.
3. Repeat on left side.
~~~~~~

~~~~~~

Theraband Triceps

1. Left arm across lap.
2. Hold band in left hand.
3. Right arm at side
4. Hold band with right hand
5. Lift hand holding band toward wall behind you.
6. Repeat to other side.

~~~~~~

Chest.

1. Band behind back & under shoulder blades, ends coming under arms.
2. Pull band straight out with both hands. Repeat 10 times.

~~~~~~

1. Wrap band above knees, holding together firmly.
2. Spread knees apart.
3. Return to start. Repeat 10 times.

~~~~~~

1. Hold both ends of band with foot in middle.
2. Knee bent toward chest.
3. Straighten knee and push foot to front.
4. Repeat up to 10 times.
5. Repeat with other leg.

~~~~~~

1. Begin in seated position.
2. Carefully rise to standing position.
3. Return to sitting.
4. Repeat slowly up to 10 times.
~~~~~~

Triceps #2

1. Lean forward in chair, with elbow bent.
2. Drop hand to side, straighten elbow.
3. Push hand toward wall behind.
4. Return to start.
5. Repeat 10 times. Repeat with other arm.

~~~~~~

Triceps

1. Right hand behind right shoulder, elbow close to head and pointed toward ceiling.
2. Left hand to ceiling.
3. Repeat up to 10 times. Repeat with left arm.

~~~~~~

Military Press

1. Pretend you are holding a broomstick behind your neck.
2. Press hand toward ceiling, slowly.
3. Return to starting position. Repeat 10 times.

~~~~~~

Sledge Hammer

1. Clasp hands over head.
2. Bring down to waist level.
3. Repeat slowly up to 10 times.

~~~~~~

Punch Out

1. Punch right arm out with left hand at shoulder level, elbow bent.
2. Switch arms, with left hand punching out, and right arm back at shoulder level.
3. Do slowly, up to 10 times with each arm.

~~~~~~
~~~~~~

Pull Lawn Mower Cord

1. Rest one forearm on knee.
2. Opposite hand reaches forward.
3. Pull back with elbow bent.
4. Repeat 10 times. Do on other side.

Kick Out (can use ankle weights if desired for next 4 exercises)

#1

1. Start with feet on floor.
2. Straighten knee, kicking foot up.
3. Repeat up to 10 times.
4. Repeat with other leg.

~~~~~~

#2

1. Begin with feet flat on floor.
2. Lift one knee toward ceiling.
3. Repeat up to 10 times. Repeat with other leg.

~~~~~~

#3

1. Stand holding back of chair.
2. Bring right leg out to side, keeping leg straight.
3. Return to starting position.
4. Repeat with left leg.
5. Alternate legs up to 10 times.

~~~~~~

Used with Permission from Mercy Parish Nurse and Health Ministry Program Health Bag
~~~~~~

John Ashley Zimmerman
About Face Church Outreach Consultants

642 Coleman Station Rd
Friedens, PA 15541

814-490-4297
john@af180.org www.af180.org

Made in the USA
Middletown, DE
21 January 2016